Jean Vanier

He Tells Me "I Love You"

The Story of the Love of God through the Bible

Paulist Press

New York / Mahwah, New Jersey

Cover and book design by Sharyn Banks
Illustrations: *A Little Sister of Jesus*

Originally published as *Je rencontre Jésus, Il me dit Je t'aime: histoire de l'amour de Dieu à travers la Bible* by Éditions Anne Sigier, an imprint of Éditions Médiaspaul since 2009
English edition copyright © 1987 by Éditions Médiaspaul

English-language edition by arrangement with ÉDITIONS MÉDIASPAUL
3965, Henri-Bourassa Boulevard
Montréal, QC, H1H 1L1   Canada

Library of Congress Control Number: 2014938295

ISBN 978-0-8091-4835-6 (paperback)
ISBN 978-1-61643-897-5 (e-book)

English-language edition published by Paulist Press
997 Macarthur Boulevard
Mahwah, New Jersey 07430
www.paulistpress.com

Printed and bound in the
United States of America

You will find in this book

This book is for you
my brother, my sister:
> It speaks of JESUS and his message
> but it is written especially to help you meet JESUS.

If you want—
stop and spend time with just one picture
one that speaks to your heart and gives you peace
or remain with one text that nourishes your heart.

> If you have difficulties
> share with a friend of JESUS
> he or she can help you a lot
> but especially pray to JESUS
> he will enlighten you.

> Little by little—it takes time—
> JESUS will reveal to you how much he watches over you
> and loves you

he calls you to follow him
so that you may do something beautiful
with your life and bear much fruit

the world needs you
the Church needs you
JESUS needs you
they need your love and your light.

Know, my brother, my sister
that there is a hidden place in your heart
where JESUS lives
this is a deep secret
you are called to live

    Let JESUS live in you,
    go forward with him!

I feel so lonely, unwanted, useless
closed up in myself
such anger and sadness in my heart
      disgusted with life and with myself.

One day I meet JESUS
　　　　he looks at me,
　　　　he smiles at me,
　　　　he touches me.
　　　　I can tell he loves me
　　　　just as I am with my difficulties

　　　　　　　　as my heart rejoices
　　　　　　　　a new source of life flows within me
　　　　　　　　a small light burns in my heart

Yes, JESUS
        I can tell
        you are really my friend
        you love me and understand me
        you trust me
                and I love you

        From now on, I will never be alone.

And JESUS guides me
he is my good shepherd
he calls me by my name
        and says:

        "Be not afraid
        in all your difficulties
        I am watching over you

                trust
        for I am with you always
        but you must make many efforts
        and go forward with me"

"I am leading you to a land of peace and of rest
 I am preparing a wonderful feast for you
 I nourish you with my Body and my Blood
 I nourish you with my heart
 I give you new strength
 I give you my spirit"

"I love each one of you so much
that I give my life for you
I want each one of you to be free and happy."

JESUS BRINGS ME INTO THE FAMILY OF GOD

He brings me to his father
who is also my father, Daddy

     Our Father

so JESUS is my big brother
     I am united to him and to the father
through the Holy Spirit which he gives me
     in baptism.

JESUS also brings me to
MARY, his Mother
she is also my mother, mommy
I love her and trust her
she is so much like JESUS.

JESUS brings me into the family of the Father
        he gives me new brothers and sisters
        in community

I am happy to be part of
        the larger family of God now
        which is spread throughout the world

                that's the Church.

And in the family of God
JESUS gives us priests
     they speak of JESUS
     they celebrate Mass, the Eucharist
     they give us the Body of JESUS to eat
       and his Blood to drink

In the name of JESUS they forgive us our sins
     they help us live the Good News of JESUS.

JESUS TEACHES ME TO PRAY

I look at him
he looks at me
    It's so good to be together!
he says: "I love you
as the Father loves me,
remain in my love"

with JESUS I am happy and relaxed.

And JESUS says to me:
> "When you pray to my Father, say:

> My Father, Our Father, daddy!
> you are so wonderful, so good, so strong!
> Oh, if only everyone could know you
> > and do what you ask!

> May your kingdom come!
> May your will be done!

See Matthew 6:9–13

"Father, I am hungry
      the world is hungry!
            I need you!
            We all need you!
            The world needs you!

Come!
Give us this day
our daily bread!"

"Father, forgive me my sins
forgive us our sins
wash all our faults away

Heal us!"

"Father, protect us
                    deliver us from evil
                    deliver us from the evil one."

Then JESUS promises me something:

"Whatever you ask the Father
        in my Name
he will give it to you
Yes, he will give it to you.
Trust!"

See John 15:16

And JESUS looks at Mary, his mother, with tenderness
        he says to her:
                "Hail, Mary, full of grace"
        I pray with him:
        "Hail, Mary, full of grace"

JESUS TEACHES ME HOW TO LIVE

JESUS looks at me lovingly
and says: "Come with me, follow me.
        We will live together"

I go with him and I see how he lives:
        He is a friend of the poor
He is so kind and gentle with the lonely ones,
        the little ones, and all unhappy people.

JESUS calls all the poor to him:

"Come to me
all you who are weary and heavy-laden
and I will give you rest
learn from me
for I am meek and humble of heart"

See Matthew 11:28

JESUS gives bread to the hungry

See Mark 6:41

Everywhere he goes, JESUS speaks of his Father
he always announces the Truth
he is really the Light of the world
he detests what is not true

**JESUS comforts the broken-hearted
he loves to live close to them**

See Luke 7:12

JESUS heals the wounded and the sick

See Luke 5:17

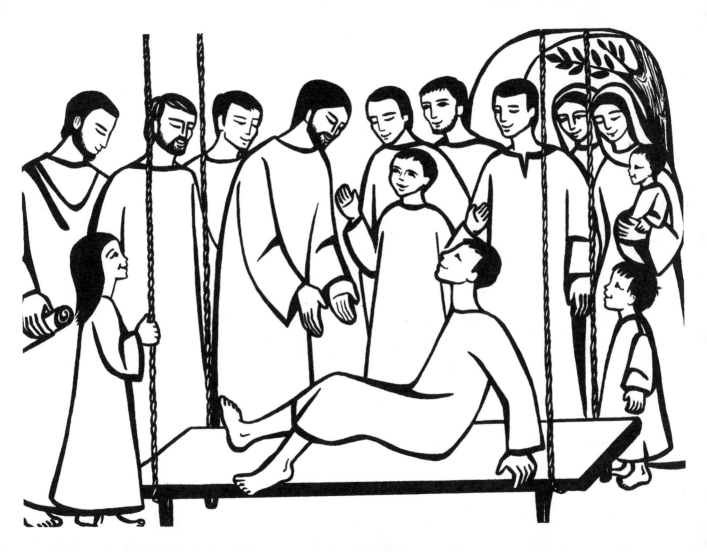

He calls little children to him

he kisses them
he blesses them
because he loves them

he says to me:
"If you do not become like one of these little ones,
        —full of trust and simplicity—
you cannot enter the Kingdom of Heaven."

See Matthew 18:2

JESUS tells me a story
to show how good his Father is
and how much he forgives us:

"There is a man who has two sons
the younger of them asks his father
for his share of money
and he leaves on a journey into a distant country.
There he wastes all his money
on loose living"

"Now when he has spent everything,
famine invades the country
he has nothing—nothing to eat
no work

  he feeds the pigs
  but he is so hungry
  he would like to eat the scraps
  that the pigs are eating

  he begins to long for his father's house"

"He decides to go back to his father
    who is waiting for him
    for he still loves his son

When he sees him coming his heart leaps with joy
    he runs to greet him
    he takes him in his arms
    and hugs him

The young son cries and says:
    Daddy, I have sinned against heaven
    and against you. I am sorry, forgive me!

        they embrace each other
        happy to be reconciled."

"The father is so happy to see his son again
that he calls for a big celebration.
Everyone rejoices
the son who was lost, has been found!
he who was dead, has come to life again!

only his older brother is angry
because he is jealous."

See Luke 15

JESUS, WHY HAVE YOU COME INTO OUR WORLD?

JESUS tells me that the Father sends him into the world
    to save everyone
    reconciling them with him
    and making them his beloved children

The Father sends JESUS
      because he loves
      all the men and women
      of the earth

he sends him to announce the good, good news:
      God loves us
      just as we are
we are no longer left alone with our difficulties,
      anguish, handicaps,
everything does not end with death
we are made to live forever
      together with JESUS
and that life begins right now.

The Father sends JESUS
     to free all men and women
     from their prisons of selfishness
          guilt
          jealousy
          oppression
          violence
          death
          evil

Yes, he comes to save us and to free us

The Father sends JESUS
       to be Peace and Reconciliation
       in a world of conflict and war
       to be compassion
       in a world of suffering and misery

JESUS comes to forgive us
     all our faults, our sins
     our cowardice and indifference
he does not come to judge or to condemn

JESUS comes
to transform our hearts
which are selfish and hard
to teach us to love and to share
and to build a world that is more just,
more beautiful, more friendly

that's the Church!

JESUS comes
> to invite all men and women
> from all countries and races
> to the great celebration of the Father

> > so that all may be ONE in him,
> > the King of Love and of Light.

And JESUS looks at me lovingly
and says: "Be like me
filled with kindness
be courageous
be my hands, my face and my heart
as I am the hands, the face and
the heart of my Father
As the Father sent me
I also send you
go announce the good news of Peace
tell everyone that God is love
liberate hardened hearts
forgive as I forgive
love as I love
struggle against the evil as I struggle
against evil."

The bishop in the name of JESUS confirms us
        for he is the father of the diocese
        he sends us forth to announce the good news
        and to serve JESUS and our brothers
        and sisters, especially the poorest
Through the sacrament of confirmation
        we receive a new strength from the Holy Spirit
        to be witnesses of JESUS

The bishop also makes new priests.

JESUS TEACHES ME HIS WAY OF LIFE: THE BEATITUDES

See Matthew 5

"Live poorly and simply
  do not seek to become rich
  find your security in me
  I am your wealth and your peace

        then you are happy
        and blessed of my Father"

"Be gentle and humble of heart
     even with those who are unkind
     or nasty to you

         then you will be happy
         and blessed of my Father"

"Do not worry when you suffer
          when you cry
     I will comfort you
     I will wipe away each one of your tears

     then you will be happy
     and blessed of my Father"

"Thirst and hunger for the kingdom of God,
Yearn that his will be done on earth as it is in heaven
pray and struggle just where you are
for a more friendly world
where the poor are honored

think of those who are suffering far away
and all those who are struggling against evil in the world
pray for them
live for them

then you will be happy
and blessed of my Father"

"Be kind with those who are lonely and rejected
        with those who are sad and in distress
        especially the poorest and the weakest
        share your life with them

        I am hidden in their hearts
        and whatever you do unto them
                you do unto me
        they will help you
        they will change your heart of stone
                into a heart of love.

                then you will be happy
                and blessed of my Father"

"May your heart be pure and transparent
like spring water

then you will be happy
and blessed of my Father"

"Seek always and everywhere to be peace-makers

then you will be happy
and blessed of my Father"

"If you are kind
if you love me and try to do what I say
      you will be laughed at
      you will be pushed
      you will be persecuted

           do not worry
           do not be afraid
           I am with you

           then you are happy
           and blessed of my Father."

I say to JESUS

"but it is hard to love, to give
        to always forgive,
        to live as you say
I try but I can't
I often fail
so quickly I become discouraged
I become lazy
and just think of myself."

JESUS smiles at me:

"Yes, for you all alone, it is impossible
but nothing is impossible for God
I am here to help you and to forgive you.
I forgive you through my priests
in the sacrament of reconciliation
In that way, you still remain my friend"

"But most important of all,
        eat my Body
        drink my Blood

    So I live in you
    and you live in me

    I give you my heart to love with
    I give you a new strength
            to struggle against evil
            in yourself and in the world"

"Without me, you can do nothing.
    with me, you will bear much fruit.

    but be patient
    remain in my love"

See John 15

"If you want to follow me
      you will suffer

but be not afraid I am with you always"

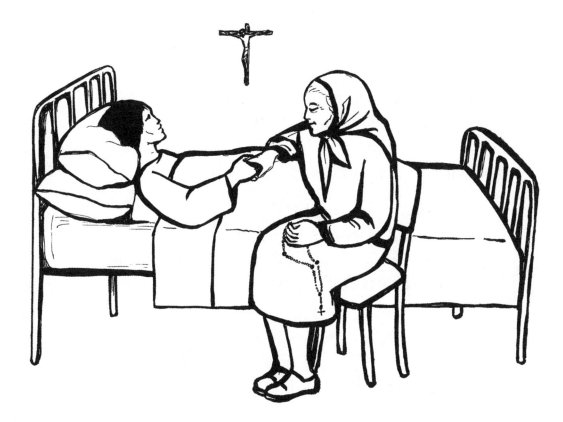

"When you die, I will welcome you forever
into the kingdom of my Father
with Mary, my Mother
and with all the children of my Father

We will live together
we will celebrate together
together we will sing praise to my Father
our hearts full of joy"

"But you must watch and pray,
　　　for Satan, the evil one
　　　tries to discourage you
　　　and to turn you away from me

　　　But I am with you to protect you;
　　　remain with me"

"Take refuge in the heart of my Father
            for he loves you
            and watches over you
            you can trust him
            for he is all-powerful in love
                    and tenderness

            he knows everything
            and not a hair falls from your head
            without his knowing it."

And JESUS tells me:

> "The kingdom of my Father
> is like a treasure hidden in a field
> it is worth selling all you have
> in order to buy it"

See Matthew 13:44

"The kingdom of my Father
        is like the smallest of all seeds:
    it grows in our hearts
            it becomes a tree
    where all the birds like to build their nests"

See Matthew 13:31

"The kingdom of my Father is like a wedding feast

to which all the poor
are invited!"

See Luke 14:5

JESUS EXPLAINS THE BEGINNINGS AND THE HISTORY OF THE WORLD

See Genesis 1

"My Father and I create all things:
light and sun
plants, leaves and flowers
fish, birds and animals"

"But most important of all
       we create man and woman

The whole universe is created for them
it is their home and their garden"

"The first man and woman,
        Adam and Eve, are tempted by the devil
        they disobey God
        they say to him: "no"
        they turn away from his love
        then they just look for pleasure in life
        they think only of themselves
        they no longer wish to serve"

See Genesis 3

"And because Adam and Eve turn away from God
and only think of themselves
they begin to fight
and their children do too

And all the men and women of the earth
begin to fight among themselves,
each one just looking for his or her own interests

there is no more love or sharing on earth
everywhere there is war, misery and hatred."

"But the Father remains faithful to his love
He has a plan for all the men and women of the earth
        which is even more beautiful
        for he loves them so much
        and he wants them to be happy.

    He is going to send them a Savior
    his only beloved Son
    to free their hearts
    and to give them new life

      and so he prepares his coming."

God chooses Noah
     he tells him to build an ark
     for himself, his family,
     and for all the animals, male and female

And God sends rain, rain, and more rain...
     it is a terrible flood!
     the whole earth is covered by water!

Only Noah and his family
     and the animals male and female
     who are in the ark are saved!

And God makes a covenant with Noah
     and with his children
     and with the children of his children
     with all the men and women of the earth
     he will not send another flood
     to destroy the earth.

See Genesis 6

But once again all the men and women of the earth
turn away from God
everywhere there is war, misery and hatred.

God chooses Abraham
a good man and just man.

with him, his wife and his children
and the children of his children
he forms a people, the Jewish people.

God makes a covenant with them.

See Genesis 15

The Jewish people suffer
     they become slaves, oppressed and humiliated.
     they cry out to God
     reminding him of his covenant.

And God hears the cry of his people
     he chooses Moses
     he sends him to liberate his people.

See Exodus 32

After many, many years,
  the Father chooses a young girl
  MARY
  to be the mother of his beloved son

  even before her birth.
  he prepares her for this
  by creating her full of grace
    and love, all pure

  she is the immaculate one.

Mary is promised in marriage to Joseph
                    a good and just man
                    who always obeys God

The Father sends to Mary a messenger,
    The angel Gabriel
    He greets her:
        "Hail Mary, full of grace,
        the Lord is with thee"

    He asks her to become
    the Mother of God
    She says "Yes"
        "I am the servant of the Lord
        Do with me what you want"

See Luke 1:23–38

The Father sends his spirit to Mary
She conceives a little child: this is JESUS
The Blessed Virgin becomes the mother of God.

Mary carries the baby JESUS within her
she goes in haste to her cousin, Elizabeth

Elizabeth is also with child in her old age
Mary goes to help and serve her.

See Luke 1:39–56

Mary gives birth to JESUS
     in a cave in Bethlehem

Joseph is there
It is Christmas

    some shepherds come to adore
the Son of God who has become a little baby

                              See Luke 2:1–20

Kings come from afar
to adore him also
and to bring him gifts.

JESUS is king of Israel
king of the whole universe

See Matthew 2

JESUS lives with Joseph and Mary
　　　　the simple family life of Nazareth

　　he works like everyone else
　　he remains there thirty years.

After these thirty years
>he leaves his home, his work and his town
>to go and announce to all people
>his message of peace and love:

>the Good News

he also works miracles.

See John 2:1–12

JESUS calls disciples and twelve apostles to join him
he asks them to leave everything and to come and follow him
he chooses them to continue his work
> to preach as he preaches
> to be good and kind as he is good and kind
> to heal as he heals
among the twelve apostles, there is Peter
JESUS chooses him to be
> the rock on which his church is built
> the first of the apostles
> the first pope

> and there is John
> whom he loves with a special love.

See Matthew 4:18–22

Today, the pope is like Peter
        he is a friend of JESUS
        the first of the bishops
        the shepherd of shepherds

he confirms the other bishops
he recalls the words of JESUS for all the Church.

Among the disciples of JESUS
        there is Mary, his mother.

she is the most attentive and the most silent
she receives his word with love and joy
she keeps all things hidden in her heart
she loves and adores.

There are also Martha and Mary
    the sisters of Lazarus

JESUS loves them very much
    he often goes to their home to rest.

See Luke 10:38

There is a woman who lives a sinful life
JESUS looks at her with tenderness and says

"I do not condemn you
go your way; from now on sin no more!"

she will not sin anymore
for she has met JESUS
and she knows she is loved infinitely.

See John 8

But others do not want JESUS
  they are frightened by his message
  they are attached to their money and their power
  they refuse to listen and to welcome his word
  they close their hearts
  they are jealous and try to trap him.

On the Thursday before the Passover

JESUS gathers the apostles
to share the meal with them

he knows it is his last meal

Before eating, he washes their feet
and becomes their servant
he says to them:

"Do this to one another"

"then you will be happy and blessed of my Father"

See John 13

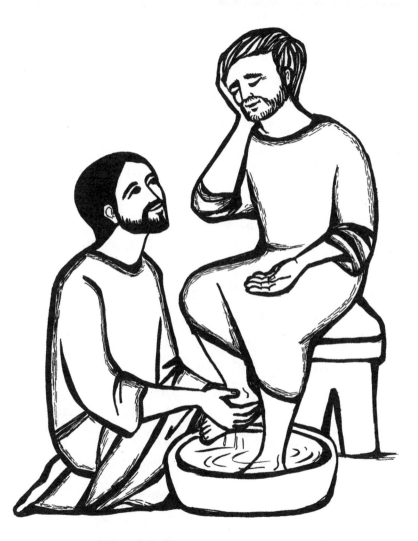

During the meal, JESUS gives to the apostles
    his Body to eat in the form of bread
    his Blood to drink in the form of wine
    a sign of his death and of the gift of his life
      it is the first Mass, the Eucharist
He says to them: "Do this in memory of me"
he makes them priests
    Then JESUS speaks to them:
      "Love one another as I love you
      this is a new commandment
      soon I will be leaving you
      but do not let your hearts be troubled!
      I will pray to the Father
      he will send you the Paraclete
        the Holy Spirit
      you will be persecuted
      but I will be with you always"

See Matthew 26
John 14:15–16

Then JESUS goes to the Garden of Olives
with Peter, James and John
        he is in deep anguish and distress
        he says to them:
                "My soul is sad unto death"

He prays: "Father, not my will but yours"

See Luke 22:40

The enemies of JESUS want to kill him
they use Judas
one of the twelve apostles
he comes with soldiers
to arrest and imprison JESUS

Judas betrays him with a kiss

Peter, the first of the apostles, is frightened
he pretends he does not know JESUS
he says:
"I do not know that man!"

and the cock crows…

from afar JESUS looks at him with tenderness

Peter weeps bitterly

JESUS forgives

See Luke 22:61

JESUS is put into prison
     he is judged
     and condemned to die on a cross
     he is struck
     and crowned with thorns
     he suffers greatly

See John 19

He carries his cross on his shoulders
to Mount Calvary

Simon of Cyrene helps him

JESUS falls a number of times
he suffers terribly

See Luke 23:26

The soldiers nail JESUS to the cross
            he is like a lamb—wounded and innocent—
            a victim to save us and to heal us

            From the cross
            JESUS gives Mary to John

            "Here is your mother"

From that moment on, John takes care of Mary
            he loves her as JESUS loves her.

See John 19

JESUS cries out: "I thirst!"
      he gives up his spirit
            he dies

      a soldier pierces his heart
      with a sword
      from the wound flows blood and water

See John 19

They take his body down from the cross
and give him to his mother
she receives him with love

Then they put the body into a tomb
sealed by a large stone.

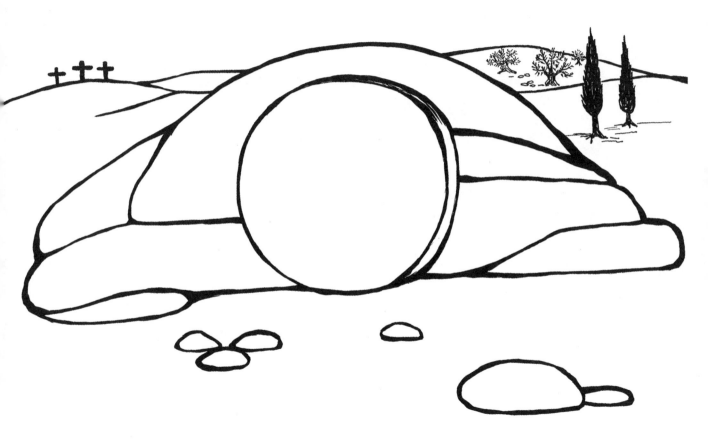

JESUS RISES FROM DEATH! ALLELUIA!

On Easter Sunday
**JESUS RISES FROM DEATH!
ALLELUIA!**

he is living now and forever!

ALLELUIA!

Early in the morning, Mary of Magdalene goes to the tomb
　　　　she is weeping
JESUS appears to her dressed as a gardener
　　　　she does not recognize him
　　　　until he calls her by her name:
　　　　　　"Mary"

　　　　she cries: "Rabboni," "Master!"
　　　　and throws herself at his feet.

See John 20:11–18

186

Later JESUS appears to his apostles
    at the lake of Tiberias
    he has breakfast with them
    then he says to Peter:
        "Peter, do you love me?"
        "Yes, says Peter, you know that I love you"
        JESUS says: "Feed my lambs"

Thus JESUS confirms Peter
    as shepherd of his Church
    as the first pope.

See John 21

On the day of Ascension

JESUS tells the apostles and disciples
to wait and pray
he is going to send them his spirit

Then he leaves them and goes to the Father.

See Acts 1

On Pentecost Sunday

        —ten days after the departure of JESUS—

        Mary and the apostles are together in prayer

        they await the promise of JESUS

    suddenly, they hear a noise

    like a violent wind

    and tongues as of fire

        appear to them

        which rest on each one of them

And they are all filled with the Holy Spirit

    a new strength rises up in them

    and they begin to proclaim in various languages:

"JESUS is the Son of God, the Savior of the world"

The Church of JESUS is born and is revealed to the world.

See Acts 2

192

The apostles filled with this new fire
go off throughout the world
to speak of JESUS
and of his good news everywhere
they baptize all those who believe in JESUS

"In the name of the Father, the Son and the Holy Spirit"

The family of God, the Church, grows in number.

Mary lives with John
        John is her priest
        until her death

Then, like JESUS, she rises from the dead
        and enters Heaven with a glorified body

                This is the Assumption!

        We too will rise with glorified bodies
                at the end of time
JESUS and Mary await us in the kingdom.

The apostles die as martyrs for JESUS
bishops replace them
      they continue to preach JESUS
      and his good news
            throughout the world
            and throughout time

      like the apostles they create
            and confirm Christian communities

      These communities are made up of
            Families—mothers, fathers
            with their children
            and also those who are not married

      some give their lives completely to JESUS

The weak, the sick, the poor, the elderly
     —all those who are suffering and lonely—
     are at the heart of these communities

they are at the heart of the Church of JESUS

     JESUS loves them with a special love
     he chooses the weak and the little ones
     to confound the strong

Their prayer touches the heart of the Father.

In the history of the Church

JESUS calls men and women
like you and me to be saints
to live the life of the Holy Spirit
        they are friends of JESUS
        friends of the poor
        and our models
they speak of JESUS and to JESUS
they speak to the poor
they are our friends
waiting for us in Heaven.

JESUS is alive
        at the heart of his Church
he remains with us and in us.

        with him we love one another
            we create community
            we learn to forgive and to celebrate
            we welcome the poor
        we give our lives for our brothers and sisters
        and we work toward creating a more friendly world
        we are the face
            the hands and the heart of JESUS

At the heart of our communities
     we pray a lot
     and offer our difficulties and sufferings
     to the Father, in union with JESUS
     so that all the men and women
     of the earth may be saved.

And all together
>with all the Church
>with all those who suffer and weep

>with Mary, mother of the Church
>mother of all the men and women of the earth

>we await the return of JESUS in his glory

>and we cry: "COME LORD JESUS, COME!"

See Apocalypse 22

"I thank you, Father
for having hidden these things
from the wise and clever,
and revealed them to little ones."

See Matthew 11:25